QUAKER VIEWS

ON

MYSTICISM

BY

MARGERY POST ABBOTT

PENDLE HILL PAMPHLET 375

About the Author

Margery Abbott is a "released Friend" currently writing and traveling in the ministry among Friends, with the support of Multnomah Monthly Meeting in Portland, Oregon. She is periodically drawn to speak or lead workshops at various venues in the United States and Britain, but her primary focus is on writing about Friends. "What Is a Friend?" is the question that informs much of her work. Who are these fervent evangelicals, unorthodox Christians (such as herself), Jewish Quakers, and occasional atheists who are among the approximately 300,000 Quakers in the world? Marge has grown in her own faith by making connections across the divides that too often separate those Friends. What started as a call to the ministry has become a leading to undertake substantial study and writing about the Religious Society of Friends. Her books on Quaker understanding of perfection and on travel in the ministry reflect the commonalities she finds when we listen with God present. Marge Abbott may be reached at marge_abbott@earthlink.net.

This is a revised and condensed version of a pamphlet originally published in the *Woodbrooke Journal,* No. 3, Summer 1998, by the Woodbrooke Quaker Study Centre in Birmingham, England. That version, entitled *Mysticism Among Friends,* may be found on the Woodbrooke website [www.woodbrooke.org.uk]. The persons interviewed by the author have granted permission to be quoted herein.

Pendle Hill Pamphlet Series Editor: Donna L. McDaniel

Address requests for permission to quote or translate to Pendle Hill Publications, 338 Plush Mill Rd., Wallingford, PA 19086-6099.
e-mail: bookstore@pendlehill.org

QUAKER VIEWS ON MYSTICISM

British Friend Val Ferguson explained mysticism and the Society of Friends to me this way: When a Danish friend of hers, testing his understanding of Quakers, asserted, "You are a peace church," she replied, "No, the peace testimony is the fruit, not the root." He then exclaimed, "Ah, you are mystics." She responded, "No, we are a peace church." Val uses this to explain the inexorable linking of inward mystical experience and outward action. Like M.C. Escher's multi-dimensional illusions, the moment you focus one way—perhaps on birds—the focus changes and the picture is full of fish. The dual images of Friends as a peace church and a group of mystics *are* inexorably linked within the Society of Friends. While we might focus on one, we only have to blink to see that the other is still present. Val and other Friends whom I interviewed, whose quotations are scattered throughout this pamphlet, conveyed a deep understanding of what Friends mean by "mysticism," even though some expressed discomfort with the word. What follows are some of their perspectives and my own on one dimension of the Escher drawing that is the Religious Society of Friends.

Mysticism is a word often used to express the experiential side of religion. In this sense it refers to the awareness of God's presence. Friends across the spectrum of liberal to evangelical react differently to this word. This pamphlet addresses the perspective of Friends within the liberal (unprogrammed) meetings in the context of my own experience and a series of interviews I conducted. After exploring some definitions of mysticism, I consider the transformative effect of the divine touch and the ways Friends have traditionally discerned the action of the Spirit in their lives. Then I weave the various strands together. Through it all runs the essential thread—that the awareness of the Spirit will result in lives that speak of justice, mercy, and compassion.

The Work of God in My Life

Over the years, more than one longtime friend has commented on how amazing the very thought was that I would be traveling among Friends in the ministry and speaking on such topics as mysticism. This work is the consequence of a mystical experience I had in my mid-forties. It is also the result of a multi-year struggle with my deep introversion and own internal fears. The Holy entered my life openly in a way I could not ignore. God comforted me after my father died, freeing both grief and joy in me. That day God set me on a path of hard work that involved a lengthy clearness process, professional counseling, and a sense of a call to ministry that has manifested both vocally and in writing. This call still seems so ironic, a sense of God's humor—I was such an unlikely character for it. At the time I had never spoken in my Meeting for Worship and was so afraid of articulating anything emotional, much less spiritual, that I would actively avoid worship-sharing groups at Yearly Meeting. I had written extensively, but only technical documents, given my training in science and professional work. I was a person who long disliked poetry, and then found myself writing reams of it.

I am a Friend who is excited and entranced by the universal compass of Friends' comprehension of the nature of human relationship with the Divine. Even as I read works of other faiths, I find it easy to spot commonalities and places where their tradition enhances my own response to God and opens up new perspectives. As a scientist, I find that the methods of modern science and modern thought can inform how I know my relationship with the people and the world around me and how that is essential to my relationship with God. I am a person of my time, not a Jew or a Greek of two thousand years ago, or even a Quaker of seventeenth-century England. Yet these all inform who I am. I cannot separate myself from them no matter how I try.

The intensity of my own experience and the lack of good ways to think about it and to reorient myself led me to read extensively among the writings of early Friends. It also led me to ask Friends today about their faith and how they understand the presence of God in their own lives—in other words, about mysticism.

Defining Mysticism

The dictionary concept of mysticism speaks of the spiritual reality not apparent to our senses of taste, smell, hearing, touch, and sight, but it also includes the occult, obscure speculation, and esoteric rites.[1] Friends' definitions focus only on the first, broader concept and circle around knowing God—Spirit, transforming power, a personal relationship with the Divine, a search for Truth—the reality of God's love, and a sense of guidance focused by discernment and waiting in the silence.

How Do You See Quaker Mysticism?

Yes, Quakerism is mystical because of the emphasis on direct experience which is at the core of mysticism. Mysticism is about experiential knowledge—knowing that is not by intellectual convincement. When experienced, it is so powerful and thus very attractive. When I have experienced all this, intellectual debate about the right choice vanished. I would call it the grail quest of Quakerism, but 99.9 percent of the time we have to live without this; therefore the real question is how we live.

There is lots of need for discernment around mystical experience—it is potentially dangerous and destructive. Ken Wilbur's writings have been valuable to me. Wilbur is a psychologist who studied Buddhist and other eastern traditions and puts our western mysticism into context. Some of what we see as religious experience is considered "gee whiz" noise in Buddhism. Paranormal experience as religious experience—"I had a vision, thus I am a mystic"—is not what is central. The cornerstone of discernment is the Fruit of the Spirit. In North Pacific Yearly Meeting, people talk about these experiences with no discernible change in how they behave towards one another; thus, this falls into "gee whiz" experience.

Since we don't recognize the authority of the Bible, etc., group discernment is essential. Clearness committees are a primary way in which we test leadings in practice. This [mysticism] is so central and potentially vitalizing, but it also has much potential for distraction and wrong-headedness. One sign of the latter is when people use it as a way of seeing their "specialness." We are sometimes reluctant to speak about mystical experiences because of the difficulty of communicating them, or out of fear of negative judgments. When someone does speak of their experience I remain unconvinced if it carries this flavor of "I am special because I have had this experience." What I eagerly listen for is sharing as testimony—"this has had a galvanizing effect upon my life. I saw things differently and could naught but act." Sharing of this sort is witnessing to our faith.

—*Maurice Warner, North Pacific Yearly Meeting, 1995.*

In the mid-1990s, I interviewed articulate Quakers from Britain, Philadelphia, and the Pacific Northwest, many holding major positions in monthly or yearly meetings. These sixty-plus Friends overwhelmingly agreed that ours is a mystical faith: we can know the mystical presence of God both individually and corporately. Several quickly and emphatically spoke of the "practical" or "ethical" nature of Quaker mysticism—the way the Inward Light leads us in our actions. A few did not describe Quakerism as a mystical religion, but instead emphasized its nature as a peace church. To these Friends, equating Quakers with mystics emphasized ecstatic experience too much. They preferred to focus on the prophetic (outward and service-oriented) elements essential to Friends.

Among those I interviewed, two definitions stand out. A Philadelphia Friend described mysticism as "the breaking through of God into every aspect of everyday life." A British Friend with a slightly different bent spoke of "a gradually transforming process, putting one's self in God's hand and letting God work on you."

Various Friends pointed out that ecstatic mystical experience *purely for its own sake*, no matter how exciting, is not what is essential to Quakerism. The importance of spiritual experiences is in their power to strengthen faith, to transform lives, or to provide clear leadings for service when properly discerned individually or in conjunction with the larger group.

Spiritual experiences can be powerful and can integrate many aspects of our life. But I also heard a real caution from several Friends that they also can lead people to what one called a "self-indulgent retreat into uplifting experiences" or to action inconsistent with Friends' core testimonies.

Various Friends mentioned discernment, mutual accountability, and testing of leadings within the group as

---

How Do You See Quaker Mysticism?

Would I call Quakerism a mystical religion? No, this is not a term I use. Mysticism is a really hard word. It is intangible. The mystical for me is not about action, it is about contemplation. Quakerism is about contemplation *and* action—that's the mixture that is actually necessary. Therefore it is not mystical. That's not to say that some Quakers are not mystical. There are those who are totally into action and think nothing about reflection and those totally into reflection and care nothing about action. That is the span from the mystic to the activist. The good thing about Quakerism is that it can cope with some of each of those. Meetings that are all activists are a pain in the neck and have no spiritual grounding … but it is the word *mystical*—what you define by *mystical*—that is the question. Divine revelations of all sorts are mystical, by definition; they are about reflection. So we should all say "yes," we've had those. Mystical experiences, intimations of that Power, they are all mystical.

Boundaries? There seem to be some from what I can tell. There are language boundaries and words I feel very uncomfortable with. Talking about "vibes from crystals" is very uncomfortable for me, going into the "new age" stuff. Although I am tolerant, I am not tolerant of that sort of thing. (I'm not actually very tolerant, but I do like to pretend I am, like every other Quaker.) That is one extreme. Also the ones who had the sudden urge to go and convert everybody—the sudden drive to action (particularly in Britain). This is also a question of culture. In this you need the discernment of Friends. This is one reason we are going back to the use of clearness committees as one of the aids for that.

—Andrew Backhouse, Britain Yearly Meeting, 1995.

---

distinctive aspects of Quaker mysticism. Others reminded us firmly of our role as a peace church and that, while numinous experience is very seductive, like chocolate, alone it is not a good diet. Ecstatic experiences alone are *not* a sign of holiness. We come to Meeting for Worship because of our hunger for God's presence and because of our desire to know what the Holy One asks of us and how we might best respond.

The presence of God is most often found in the still, small voice, the quiet leadings that are easily overlooked in the throes of daily life. One Friend noted, "God comes to us in everyday struggles and disciplines. These are more reliable than the peak experiences that are only discerned afterwards. Corporate mysticism allows for the engagement of the intellect as well as the emotions. Quakerism is not a religion of pure feelings."

Thus, mysticism as known within the Society of Friends is our awareness of (or belief in) God's presence, individually and in the corporate Meeting for Worship, an awareness that results in a changed perception of the world and a willingness to be guided by the Spirit, the Inward Light, the Christ Within. Quakerism is strongly prophetic—it is about listening for that which is eternal and bringing the divine word to the world. We cannot forget that living out the will of God is the core of our faith.

The Mysticism of Rufus Jones

In the first half of the twentieth century, Rufus Jones made Friends conscious of mysticism and popularized the use of that term among Friends. Jones had a clear vision of a positive mysticism, "an immediate, intuitive knowledge of God... or consciousness of a Beyond or of a Divine Presence" which inevitably led to service. His understanding was that Quakers were inheritors of the positive mysticism of the early Christians, John and Paul in particular, and not in the tradition of the *apophatic* (employing the *via negativa*) mysticism of St. John of the Cross. Jones's work is full of optimism about the possibility of changing the world and delight in his relationship with God. He looks to "at-one-ment" with God, more than the sacrificial atoning death of Christ Jesus. While many students of Quaker history disagree with Jones either about the influence of European mystics on early Friends or his neglect of apophatic mysticism, his influence on contemporary liberal Quakerism is quite real and strong.

Jones was adamant that mystical experience is not an end in itself and does not lead us to a quietist stage, but rather into a genuine mission in the world—the voice of Christ within does not bring a plan, but rather a vital urge to life. Rather than detailed instructions, guidance is a slowly ripening fruit. Jones mentions yoga, Zen Buddhism, and other disciplines, but they do not appeal to him—they are "too doctrinaire and too remote from life to be satisfactory ways into the heart of divine reality." Jones is more interested in preparation through appreciation of beauty, learning how to love, and cultivation of the fruits of the Spirit. "What counts most is the fellowship and influence of spiritually contagious persons who, beholding as in a mirror the glory of the Lord, unconsciously transmit that Life." He describes "expectation" as another name for faith and proposes these stages in "the progress of the soul":

- concentration, an essential discipline;
- active meditation or "recollection";
- contemplation where the soul is no longer focused on an object but experiences a quickening and "unification of all the powers of the spirit," which he also spoke of as "activity fused with the peace and serenity of receptivity."[2]

Jones goes on to emphasize that:

> [Mystics] say with almost one accord that no vision of God is adequate that remains private and is not translated into life and action. The true test of an inner vision, they all insist, is the impact it gives toward pushing back the skirts of darkness and making the area of the Kingdom of God wider.[3]

During the course of the twentieth century, mysticism struggled to find its place within the growing scientific, practical, and rationalist emphasis of modern thought. As a result, much Quaker discussion of mysticism has regularly been modified by terms such as "rational" and" ethical" in order to emphasize the importance to Friends of engaging with the problems of the world. Jones would agree with the centrality of such work in the world and devoted much effort to the founding of the American Friends Service Committee. Jones has shaped liberal Friends' views more than any other individual.

How Do You See Quaker Mysticism?

Early Quakerism, in my reading, was undeniably and deeply mystical. Fox admonished Friends to "be still" and "wait" for direct guidance. People came into assemblies of Quakers to have a direct experience of God. Being centered, open, and in direct touch with God is a hard condition to maintain over time. As Quakerism has developed, it has settled into being more rational and more defined by tradition and less ecstatic and mystical. Mysticism (which I define as a direct sense of the presence of God) is still present among Friends and always has been, but is less of a defining factor.

Regarding discernment: my experience, what I know of the experience of contemporary mystics, and my reading all indicate that discerning the voice of God is difficult and confusing. Mystics are greatly aided by having a supportive, experienced community that can assist them in discernment. And the Society of Friends is greatly aided when we can help people from going off in our name on what appear to be grossly misguided tangents.

On the other hand, it is a ludicrous oxymoron to ask if there are boundaries to acceptable spiritual *experience* in the context of Quakerism. How can we put boundaries on experience? God comes to people in amazing and unexpected ways: A burning bush! An angel telling a young virgin she is going to have a child! A vision of an ocean of darkness overlaid by an ocean of light! Experience happens and we try to interpret what happened and discern what we are supposed to do. If we put boundaries on what we can *experience*, we have to close ourselves to the promptings of the Spirit altogether, lest they come to us in ways we have, a *priori*, decided are unacceptable. Moses wasn't expecting a burning bush; he certainly wasn't wild about going off to Egypt to confront the Pharaoh; and his neighbors probably thought he was a crackpot. We can only imagine how Mary's family responded to "Uh, Mom—I'm pregnant, but don't worry, God is the father." What if Moses had decided never to listen to talking bushes? Or if Mary didn't sit on her window sill? What if Fox regarded the oceans of darkness and light as hallucination to be feared and denied?

-Patricia McBee, Philadelphia Yearly Meeting, 1996.

The Transforming Work of the Spirit

I do not know whether George Fox or other seventeenth century Friends would have considered themselves mystics—that was probably not a relevant question at the time, although it has been a matter of debate for at least fifty years. Fox's language is full of the visionary and poetic. One of my favorite phrases of his is "I came up through the flaming sword into the paradise of God." Fox, without a doubt, knew of the direct presence of the Inward Christ in his life, inspiring his words in worship, transforming him, and guiding his daily actions. Fox so integrated the Bible into his life that it is almost impossible to separate his words from the biblical expression that permeates his language. He addressed questions of sin and evil head on and believed that human beings could live out the kingdom of heaven on earth if they heard and followed the voice of the Light of Christ within their hearts.[4]

Fox's language and experiences have become familiar to me in the past few years as I have sought to respond to my own strong, transforming mystical experiences. Images come to me full of life: images of communion wine glasses in the heart of a gathered meeting, images of neon spirals that mark my path toward God in community. These vivid images express the brilliance, the joy, and the glory of God's work in us, but I have also struggled against the change they imply. I have come to know the work involved if I am to live out more fully the love that God has shown me.

Many early Friends experienced strong visions and dreams that expressed not only joy, but also the deep pain, struggle, and transformation that may accompany opening into the Inward Light. The Cross was very present in their lives. Accepting the work of Christ within them often required a reaming out, a stripping, a tormented facing of their own sinful nature. This kind of conversion is not just a relic of the past, but is a vital path today for some of us as we accept the power of God in guiding our lives. The process of being transformed from a life centered in human will to a life centered in the Light can be as sudden and full of struggle as it was for a number of early Friends. Yet my interviews suggest that today it is more often experienced as a slower, easier process.

How most modern Friends experience the presence of God is unclear since we so rarely speak of it. In my conversations, reading, and interviews, the intense struggles and strong transformations so often mentioned in early Quaker journals are the exception rather than the typical experience of the Spirit today. The Light guides us, comforts us, opens our hearts, and gradually changes us. We may sense a "coming home" upon entering Meeting for Worship. We may know God's power and mystery on a mountain hike, in the glory in a sunset, or the perfect beauty of dew on a rose. This knowing is healing if we allow it to be.

Even for those of us who have been sharply and radically transformed, we most often know God's guidance in the still, small voice, the nudges in our hearts, or the seemingly fortuitous phone call. Many gentle guides appear along our path if we stop to notice them. This sense of leading is in accord with the thinking of those who separate the workings of the Inward Light from the numinous and remind us that God's guidance is most central.

Speaking About the Divine Encounter

Speaking about the work of the Spirit in our lives is inherently difficult. Powerful inward experiences are beyond any possible language, although poetry comes closest to

---

How Do You See Quaker Mysticism?

How do I define *mysticism*? I don't. I do see Quakerism as mystical. The mystical is rooted in individual or corporate experience of God, not particular belief. This raises the question: How do you recognize a true mystical experience? It comes back to authority and the role of the meeting. If the individual experience is so at variance from the meeting, it is somehow unacceptable.... There should be echoes in the community and in reading. There are boundaries, which means some people are outside the boundaries, but I have no experience to draw on here.

Alongside showings of the [British] Quaker Tapestry, Barry and Jill Wilsher (founders of the Quaker Peace Caravan) did a show around Britain that included a quote from Will Warren, who worked in Northern Ireland, that he hoped he would have been able to love the Commandant at Auschwitz. When we hosted the show, a Friend in my local Meeting who had lost many family members in the Holocaust felt that she could not do this, and found the quote unacceptable. Her experience is not mine and I cannot blame her for this, but I do see this love of the individual as essential. We British Friends can be so sheltered from the violence and horror that seeking God in others is just sweetness and light. We *need* to understand what startling and powerful things we are about—but that what we are asking of people and saying is possible.

-Peter Eccles, Britain Yearly Meeting, 1995.

---

allowing some sense of the experience to flow in a way that resonates in the soul, as long passages of poetry in the Bible attest. Yet verbal communication is part of what builds a community and may be part of what God asks us to share with one another. So we use language to speak of that which is beyond all words. And we react to one another's choice of words, sometimes with anger. Some Friends state that only Christian language can be used to speak of the mystical; others find Christian language painful to hear. I suspect that all words about the touch of the Holy Spirit are difficult to use and that almost any words one chooses will be uncomfortable for some people.

When speaking of mystical experience, language becomes quite slippery. The absence of an easily understood vocabulary and the natural hesitation to speak about spiritual experiences make this topic especially difficult. On the whole, interviewees conveyed a reality that God speaks to humanity in multiple ways and touches each person in a manner unique to that individual. Some spoke, as did a Philadelphia Friend, of a unitary experience that was clear, confirming, and foundational to her faith where, she said,

> I knew the love of God—a pure gift, totally unexpected, out-of-time. Another time, at the 1967 World Conference—while shaking hands with a Kenyan woman, I had an amazing feeling of wholeness, connectedness, and love of God.

These experiences were unmistakable and have remained strong with that Friend all her life. Although it felt impossible to articulate, she has never questioned the reality of

God's presence to her in that moment.

For others, the silence of the unprogrammed worship is filled with the possibility of spiritual experience and this is part of the lure of Quakerism. A Friend from the Pacific Northwest said, "Yes, many have had such experiences. No, it is not easy to speak of them. It is exciting to read of others' descriptions of their experiences." He was certain that these experiences are not in isolation and do not exist simply for our own edification. "Mysticism is the direct contact with the spiritual. Quakerism adds obedience, service, and action." Mysticism is not an abstract, free-floating experience.

Speaking of such experiences can seem too risky. The fear might be that when we speak of a voice that comforts or instructs us, we will be judged "crazy." We may fear that when we offer what is precious to our soul it will be trampled in some way or misinterpreted. It is crucial to a healthy Meeting for Worship to have caring people with the experience and sensitivity to nurture the glimmers of the Spirit in those around them as well as to provide a container, witness, and discerning heart for more powerful experiences of God.

The work of the Spirit in our hearts has infinite dimensions. Profound mystical experiences come in many forms; there is no way to say how God might touch some-one or how each of us may best be taught the way of com-passion. We do, as Friends, have clear expectations about what is acceptable in the community and in our worship together. We offer people a place to listen quietly for the still, small voice and for other manifestations of the Spirit rising out of the silence. In paying attention to the Spirit, we find that words are present to minister to the whole. We know the Light as our inward teacher whose voice guides our lives and undergirds our concerns for peace and justice. God is present as we do business together with searching open hearts. The stillness of worship nurtures the intuitive stillness of the soul within all people; it is not limited by personality or upbringing.

Chanting, singing, physical sharing of the sacramental bread and wine, movement, or listening to a powerful sermon can all open hearts to the work of the Spirit. Some people find they need multiple sources and ways to open themselves to God's work. Being aware that private or individual spiritual practices are not necessarily the same as the community worship is part of the process of understanding who we are as Friends. Integrity draws us to the inward state where no contradictions exist when we are responsive to the Light. In the Spirit we can become aware that many ways bear fruit compatible with the teachings of Jesus.

Unspoken Expectations and Cautions

What are the unspoken expectations among Friends about their communal practice of mysticism and about the way individuals speak of or act in response to mystical experiences? As can be seen from the passage on page 19, this is one of the more difficult questions for liberal Friends. The propensity of liberal Friends to say "no" when asked if there are "boundaries" to mystical experience makes many evangelicals nervous about mysticism.

The tradition of unprogrammed worship as it evolved in the twentieth century holds strong appeal for intellectuals and introverts as well as for those who see themselves as "intuitives." The expectation of quietness sets unspoken "rules" about behavior in worship and seems to limit awareness of the Spirit to a silent, sometimes personal practice. Yet it is possible to think about the outwardly different, but in many ways familiar, forms of mysticism that are present in the charismatic churches where many

---

How Do You See Quaker Mysticism?

YES! Quakerism is a mystical religion. I define mysticism as an individual's direct experience of the Divine. Sometimes these experiences are tender leadings rather than something that knocks us over. We need to give credence to the uplift present in nature and to those who sense love in every cell of their body for their family. By giving credence here we open the possibility for the transforming bolt of lightning. If we deny the reality of lighter mystical experiences, we close off the door to the other.

Discernment: By definition mystical experiences defy the ability to talk about them as does orgasm. To put such experience in the form we call language is never adequate. Attempting discernment might rob them of the mystical qualities. There are times when it is right to put pure mystical experiences into words, but they are incredibly difficult to express.

In terms of boundaries, unfortunately, yes, they exist. We are expected to have them [mystical experiences] quietly and alone. Even in Meeting for Worship we are expected to be essentially alone—not singing, dancing, quaking, speaking in tongues, there or elsewhere. The line between the mystical and being crazy is ill-defined. Mystical experience is not supposed to draw someone else into the experience. What is now unacceptable used to be early Christian expressions and we as twentieth century Quakers have put restrictive limits on our experiences.

-Margaret Sorrel, North Pacific Yearly Meeting, 1995.

---

varieties of expression are experienced as the direct divine touch. For the charismatic, the Holy Spirit is experienced directly in the speaking in tongues, in movement, and in deep personal relationship with Jesus Christ—ways that are largely unacceptable in the context of unprogrammed Meeting for Worship. These more emotional, outward, and concretely oriented expressions are distrusted by many liberal Friends and listed by some as outside their understanding of mystical experience. Yet they show many underlying similarities to Friends' ways.

Good mental health requires being able to function within our own culture. Some interviewees noted that the line between the mystical and mental instability is difficult to define and varies with the individual, the situation, and even the culture. While a true mystical experience may lead someone to deal with difficult issues and face uncomfortable situations, the inward touch of God is healing, not destructive to the individual.

Many interviewees cautioned about the need for discernment in understanding mystical experiences, particularly the more vivid ones, and the resultant behavior. "Like sexual experience, no [mystical] experience can be right which demeans another or demeans oneself."[5] Or, as an English Friend said,

> Yes, there are boundaries, e.g., no speaking in tongues. In Great Britain, most people would be expected to be decently quiet about [mystical experiences]. Psychosomatic manifestations are wrong. It is okay if the experience is inward and quiet; if loud, it shifts into mental instability.[6]

Friends had another significant caution about mysticism, particularly when it is experienced as visions, voices, or other paranormal expressions. It is easy to get caught up and believe that having visions makes one special in some way. As some Friends point out, when we begin to distinguish those who have visions as somehow better than others or to dismiss the gentle, unspectacular ways in which God works in most people's lives, we have lost the way.

Occasionally Friends warned that experiences can be sick or twisted—Hitler claimed to have mystical experiences, one noted. But these possibilities were considered the exception. The fact that visions and other similar experiences can be induced by drugs is in itself a warning that discernment is needed to recognize when they are truly of God. Deeply experienced contemplatives from Buddhist masters to Teresa of Avila have seen the traps in focusing on and seeking after the numinous when visions are not the true goal. Visions can never be an end in themselves. They only have value when they speak of Truth and of God and transform lives in the way of compassion.

Discernment and Testing

The need for discernment increases as we start to respond to these inner experiences and take action. How do we know when it really is God as the Inward Teacher, not Aunt Sadie who always told us we had to behave? When is it divine guidance? When is it our desire for glory or revenge, or some other voice that distracts us from the right path? Knowing the immediate presence of the Spirit and knowing that this presence can guide us and give direction to our lives—that is really essential.

How Do You See Quaker Mysticism?

What about discernment? Julian of Norwich says that her visions are not important. I understand her as meaning that actually that sort of experience is not important unless it becomes part of the transformation. The discernment is by the fruits. The means of communication are not important; what is important is the recognition that God is communicating with you, then acting on it. When God communicates with me in pictures, they are always pictures of Jesus. This tends to affect my understanding of Christ.

When I was trying to decide whether to apply for the job at Homerton, the job that I now hold, I was not about to jump in. My guidance had been incredibly weak on this matter. So I said to God:

> These promptings have been incredibly weak. I think you
> mean me to go ahead, but I quite realize I could have got
> it wrong, so it really is your responsibility as well as my
> responsibility that I get it right.

So what I decided was that I would go ahead and apply, but I said to God, "If I get it wrong, I will kill you." So what does God do but flash up a picture of the cross, saying "you've already done that."

One day I was rushing late to get the train to a meeting, praying to God that "if you really love me there will be a parking space," and at the station there was a parking place right in front and a message in my head "NOW, do you believe it!" OK, God.

I don't pray for parking spaces, I try to go where God wants me to go. And if God wants me to be there, God makes it possible.

It is probably wrong for Friends to seek out mystical experiences because they are seeking for the wrong thing. What experience they have should be within the context of the Discipline, our meetings' belief in right ordering, and our lives lived according to the testimonies. If some sort of religious experience leads us to believe we should do something not in accord with our testimonies, then perhaps we need to think again, come back again and again to this, look it up in the Scriptures.

-Janet Scott, Britain Yearly Meeting, January 1995.

Because our egos and our past can get in the way of hearing what is truly of God, we rely on a process of discernment. *Discernment* comes from the Latin word *discernere*, meaning to "separate," "distinguish," "determine," "sort out." In classical spirituality, discernment means identifying what spirit is at work in a situation: the Spirit of God or some other spirit. Discernment is "sifting through" our interior and exterior experiences to determine the origin. Discernment helps us understand the source of a call, to whom it is directed, its content, and what response is appropriate. It also helps us learn if one is dodging a call, deaf to a call, or rejecting a call.[7]

The community has an important role to play in this discernment as it nurtures the individual's relationship with the Holy Spirit and enables those who are called to certain work or ministry. This role has always been central to Friends; that was confirmed by most of those I interviewed. The community's role is found in several aspects, most importantly the Meeting for Worship, the business meeting, and clearness committees. Many Friends emphasized that what is important about the mystical—the interaction of God and humanity—is not so much that it happens, but the way in which it is expressed in individual behavior and in the community.

Just as the Light has multiple dimensions, so does discernment. God most frequently touches and guides us in very gentle ways—I describe them as "nudges on the heart." Discerning these nudges is most often personal and inward. Often it involves clearing the mind and heart of other concerns and encouraging the ego to get out of the way so that we might hear clearly that still, small voice.

At times we may be deeply shaken. In worship, we may find our hearts pounding and our bodies quaking as words rise up in us to be spoken. This physical measure has long been one of the tests for vocal ministry, along with a more intellectual consideration of whether the message is more truly a personal one to be considered in the silence or for the whole group, or whether the message is for another time and place and to be seasoned in the heart. Again, the discernment process is inward and personal, yet occurs in the context of the worshiping community and is nurtured by that body.

At other times when our souls are deeply touched by God we may find that we are called in some way. We may be called to change the nature of our living, to transform our own behavior. We may be called to work among immigrants, marry a loved one, stop acts of hatred, refuse to fight, or teach in unexpected places. It may be experienced as a personal call or a call to gather others into a particular work or to account for their behavior. While at times discernment may be individual, recognition and understanding the dimensions of a call from God often benefit greatly from the wisdom of the community. Depending on the nature of the call, the advice of respected individuals, a clearness committee, or the meeting as a whole gathered to conduct business may be involved.

Early Friends were quite clear about the need for discernment to know truly whether behavior and spoken messages were of God or not. They had a number of tests, a number of aids for themselves in this process. Early Friends knew the ways in which individuals can deceive themselves and so they regularly tested leadings, either informally with others whose discernment they trusted, or in the larger body of the Meeting for Worship for Business.

In her Pendle Hill pamphlet, *Spiritual Discernment*,[8] Patricia Loring identifies a number of signs used by early Friends. They may be paraphrased as follows:

• Fruit of the Spirit. The "fruit" referred to is described in Galatians 5:22, 23, as "love, joy, peace, patience, kindness, generosity, faithfulness, gentleness, and self-control" (New RSV). These are the marks of a life lived authentically in the Spirit. The presence or absence of these fruit suggests the presence or absence of the Spirit of God.

• "Taking up the Cross." By this, early Friends meant responding to a leading that is contrary to our own willful desire, our own greed, our own egocentricity. The Cross is the call to obedience to divine will and leadings. Early Friends were clear that God's will does not always coincide with human desire. A true leading stays with us and is not impatient of obstacles, hard work, or other difficulties.

• Unity and the nature of our spiritual community together. As we "wait on the Lord" together, we can come to know our love for one another and for the world and we can come to know how that love should be acted out. "Love, joy, and unity can be signs of grounding in the realm of the Spirit and the capacity to bear its fruit in deeds of love." This is most visible in the unity of the gathered business meeting.

• Consistency with the Bible. Friends have always understood that the "Truth"—the Way of God—will not vary with different times and different cultures. If we read the Bible in the spirit in which it was written, the truth will still shine through, and a true leading will be consistent with what is revealed in its pages.

•   Inner Peace. "Feeling at peace with a decision or an outcome, even if it is not what one sought or hoped for, even if it calls for considerable hardship or change," has long been a test for Friends. This inner peace is not a simple question of being comfortable with a decision—although that might be the case. Rather, it is a deep inner feeling of rightness that can underlie even a very difficult decision. "Peace," as referred to by early Friends, is generally not related to a specific outcome, but to faithfulness in taking the actions required.

The "fruit of the Spirit" is a kind of short-hand way to describe the expectation of Friends that inward experience and outward behavior are intimately connected. The ethics of the Sermon on the Mount are also a key element. Living out the testimonies is another way of expressing such an expectation. Quaker historian Hugh Barbour describes the tests early Friends applied to leadings as moral purity (not being enslaved by self-will), the self-consistency of the Spirit over time, and inward unity.[9]

The multitude of differing tests used by early Friends indicates to me the fact that none is perfect. One will be right for a given person at a given time. And all have their limitations and can be manipulated or abused if someone so desires. An example of a simple limitation would be a meeting in which members have very similar backgrounds. While thus it can be relatively easy to come to unity, the meeting may miss important dimensions that could come forth in a more diverse group.[10]

Weaving the Strands Together

For me, mystical experiences are vivid and I struggle with God, resisting strongly the transformation opened to me. I have come to learn that God's voice is most often gentle and quiet as I come to understand anew the process of discernment. I am called to vocal messages, a personal ministry, a re-orienting of my life to one centered in God. My soul is comforted and nurtured. A number of things are crucial to me as I am touched by experiences beyond my comprehension:

I need others with whom I can talk. They may have had similar experiences or simply be willing to listen with openness and sensitivity. Without others to listen, I find myself drawn into circles that can easily twist inward. What is right is to reach outward.

I find many guides in Friends' writings, the Bible, Buddhist writings, and elsewhere. These teach me of other ways to respond and help me recognize what is my own selfishness or fear and what is the Way for me.[11]

I keep asking myself, "What difference does it make?" I look for what each internal leading or vision or nudge means in my relationships with others, in how I behave, and in the work I do. Sometimes a leading is clear and strong and I have no question what I must do. At other times I need to sort through the mess of thoughts and impulses in my head before I am clear.

Internal "markers" are quite important for me. A number of very personal markers tell me it is time to pay attention to what I am doing and to look for ways to respond. Some "markers" that warn me of the need to change are a tendency to withdraw from people, the desire to hide, a feeling that the world is getting in the way of living, anger at the small obstacles in life, or nightmares. Then there are the "markers" of God's presence—times of spontaneous prayer, a sense of overflowing joy, a deep sureness about an action or words even when they don't make sense, a word or phrase that jumps at me out of a page, or a book that begs to be read. When this happens, all I can do is delight and respond. Each person attending to the Inward Teacher will find his or her own internal markers.

The Individual and the Corporate

Both the community of Friends and the accounts of our Quaker past are essential strands in the web of mysticism. The deeper I go on this journey with God, the more I am aware of how easy it is to be drawn in strange directions that can end in harm and the more I desire to walk in the Light. In the confusion that is all too often there for me, I need guidance from others and a structure to hold on to. Friends' radical understanding of the gospel creates a structure for me out of which I can act more clearly and surely.

Meeting for Worship for Business is one place where we practice being mystics. As we do our corporate business we learn and practice ways by which we can bring a sense of the Holy into everyday life—in short, how to live our faith. Worshipful conduct of business brings us back to the core of what we are about as Friends, namely knowing that God can be present to us, that God can guide us, and that we can know wholeness and holiness.

The stillness of unprogrammed worship holds a tremendous power. The witness of jointly waiting on God—waiting for openings of the Inward Light—can force us singly and as a group to step outside the ordinary limits of culture, tradition, and individual perspectives. The encounter with the Inward Light is by nature transforming—whether it be a gentle chipping away over the years or a sudden unmistakable shock to the system, no one can walk away from a true meeting with God unmarked. In that experience lies the grounds for Friends' connection with all people of faith.

The message of early Friends is still radical in the twenty-first century. It is expansive enough to enfold multiple aspects of modern culture, drawing from them an added richness. Yet the radical nature of the message that at its core must be continually refreshed by the encounter with the Seed/Inward Light/Christ in each generation, demands that we remain apart from our culture and time in ways that are not always easy to see at the moment.

Principles of Quaker Mysticism

Another strand connects the Christian and universal aspects of my faith. The Catholic Church's long tradition of mysticism was generally the province only of monastics, yet Friends have been described as practicing the monastic sense of discipline and attention to the inner life while living in the secular world. William Johnston, a Catholic who has spent years in Japan studying the religions of Asia, describes:

> the rise of a new school of mysticism within Christianity. Slowly but surely a new mystical contemplation is coming to birth. It is different from traditional Buddhist or Hindu mysticism .... It is growing year by year .... [12]

Johnston's new way comes close to describing the reality of liberal Friends today. I modify his words somewhat and add an essential point of Quakerism—our belief that God can guide our daily lives—in using Johnston's approach to describe modern liberal Quaker mysticism:

• The Light, God, Spirit, is available to all people in all times and all places.

• The nature of the mystical, of God, of the Infinite, is ultimately indescribable. Thus the response is often one of naked faith and trust without a clear assurance such as that provided in scripture.

• The unity of nature, humanity, and God involves a holistic approach blending heart, mind, body, and soul or the spiritual, psychological, physical, and intellectual. Self-knowledge and emptying of the self are part of entering into this unity.

• God reaches out and touches us each in a way we can hear, experience, know the nature of Love. No one path is right for all.

• There is a still, small voice that can guide us individually and as a community. Listening for it and responding are central to a Spirit-led life.

The above words offer one way of considering how Friends blend the Christian and non-Christian ways in their faith. In the silence and in the absence of the creedal or ritual demands found in most churches, liberal Friends have pursued or brought with them into our meetings the insights of psychology, the practices of Asian meditation, rituals associated with the rhythm of the seasons, and affinity with the natural world as well as the traditions and faith of various Christian churches. In the silence and in the absence of creed, these multiple influences are blending in complex ways that offer great potential and openness to the possibilities of life in tune with the Eternal.

The description of Quaker mysticism based on Johnston's work speaks to me for several reasons. It acknowledges that the Inward Light is available to all people and that the Spirit will offer guidance for the way we live. This model also recognizes the variety of ways that people experience God and the multiple kinds of experiences that one person may have over time. At times deep worship for me is full of images; at other moments it is a contemplative silence impossible to explain. When God touches my heart, this touch affects all of who I am and what I do, even when I find it difficult to act in accord with what I know. I can identify with the early Friends who knew without a doubt that the Inward Light of Christ shows us our sins, as well as the way out of sin. And I cannot separate Quaker mysticism from its Christian roots, even as I delight in the infinite ways God works among humankind.

Conclusion

These past dozen years have been a process of coming to know God, to know myself, to be open to change, and to do the hard work essential to deep transformation. As I am opened to experience the presence of the Holy, I come to know mysticism as a catalyst in the process of developing a relationship with God. Out of this divine relationship grows new relationships with people that reflect the nature of how I know God. For me, these relationships with the Giver of Life and with those around me mean several things:

• Transformation. In the joy and the comfort that God showers on me comes an awareness of great freedom and potential in my life and a sense of where I fall short of what is possible. In knowing God's compassion for me, I see how I can respond to others in a similar way and, in doing so, now I can step out of the confines of fear and the limits of old habits. The "fruit of the Spirit" is vibrant in the light of mystical experience.

- Communication. For whatever the reason, I have visions-images that tell me something of my relationship with God. Even more importantly, they give me words to share with others—something of what is ultimately inexpressible.

- Discernment. At the same time that great possibilities are opened in me, I become aware of the strength of fear, pain, anger, and so much else that holds me to old patterns and keeps me from realizing those possibilities. I use my own internal markers and create a simple "guidebook" to help me sort through the confusion that at times still can swamp my head. I have found a growing circle of people whose sense of compassion and integrity helps me sort through the muck and discover my right direction. The third piece in discernment is my meeting. Over the years it has taught me about trust, love, patience, joy, kindness, generosity, faithfulness, gentleness, and self-control, and it continues to teach me and assist me.

- Testimony. Testimonies are integral to the Society of Friends. They speak of how we live our faith and give us an understanding of the active nature of a life centered in God. They have always been important to me and I have tried to live as faithfully as I could. As my relationship with God grows and changes me, the testimonies take on a richer focus and become clearer as a natural witness of God's work in our lives and a way of sharing that witness.

Endnotes

[1] *Mystic:* a person who seeks by contemplation and self-surrender to attain unity with the Deity or the absolute and so reach truths beyond human understanding. *Mystical:* 1) relating to mystics or mysticism; having spiritual symbolic or allegorical significance that transcends human understanding; of or relating to ancient religious mysteries or to other occult rites. 2) inspiring a sense of spiritual mystery, awe, and fascination. *Mysticism:* beliefs or state of mind characterizing mystics; vague or ill-defined religious or spiritual belief, especially as associated with belief in the occult. *Oxford Concise English Dictionary,* 1999, p. 944. *Mysticism* is also defined as "obscure or irrational speculation." *Webster's Seventh New Collegiate Dictionary,* Springfield, Massachusetts: G. & C. Merriam Co., 1971.

[2] Rufus Jones, *The Testimony of the Soul.* New York: The Macmillan Co., 1936, pp. 29-31.

[3] Jones, p. 44.

[4] George Fox regularly spoke of "hearing" the Light and equated it with the voice of Christ. See Lewis Benson, *Catholic Quakerism.* Philadelphia: Philadelphia Yearly Meeting Book Services, 1966, p. 28.

[5] Interview, Elizabeth Allen of Britain Yearly Meeting, January 1995.

[6] Interview with a member of Britain Yearly Meeting who chose not to be identified, 1995.

[7] Suzanne G. Farnham, Joseph P. Gill, R. Taylor McLean, and Susan M. Ward, *Listening Hearts: Discerning Call in Community.* Harrisburg, Pennsylvania: Morehouse Publishing, 1991, p. 23. (The authors note their debt to Quakerism in developing their book.) A footnote refers to John Carroll Futrell's "Ignatian Discernments" and his discussion of the Ignatian concept of *diakrisis pneumaton,* "discernment of Spirits," *Studies in Spirituality of Jesuits,* Vol. 2, no. 2. St Louis: American Assistancy Seminar on Jesuit Spirituality, 1969, p. 47.

[8] Patricia Loring, *Spiritual Discernment: The Context and Goal of Clearness Committees.* Wallingford, Pennsylvania: Pendle Hill Pamphlet (No. 305), 1992.

[9] Hugh Barbour, *The Quakers in Puritan England*. Richmond, Indiana: Friends United Press, 1964, pp. 119-122.

[10] Adapted from Loring. See also Paul Lacey, *Leading and Being Led*. Wallingford, Pennsylvania: Pendle Hill Pamphlet (No. 264), 1985.

[11] Some of my guides: Sandra Cronk, Pema Chodron, Richard Foster, the gospels, Ephesians, Psalms 40, 42, 139, Isaiah 41-43, Brenda Clift Heales and Chris Cook, Rachel Hicks, Lucretia Mott, John Punshon, Janey O'Shea, Ignatius, Gerald Hughes (*God of Surprises*), Emma Bragdon (*Call of Spiritual Emergency*), Adam Curle, Morton Kelsey.

[12] William Johnston, *Letters to Contemplatives*. Maryknoll, New York: Orbis Books, 1992. On pages 3-6 Johnston proposes a "third way" of Christian mysticism. The essential characteristics of this third way are:

> First of all, whereas traditional Christian mystical teaching has been geared to monks and nuns and professionally religious people, the new mysticism appeals also to the laity….Now we see that contemplation is not the preserve of a few but open to all and sundry….Secondly, this new mysticism speaks a different language….The new mystical theology, on the other hand, is holistic….And that brings me to a third characteristic of the new mysticism: emphasis on posture and breathing.
>
> A fourth characteristic of the new mysticism is its emphasis on faith. Needless to say, all prayer and mysticism are based on radical faith: but here I speak of a faith that is divorced from words and letters and thought. We call this pure faith, naked faith, dark faith….A fifth characteristic of the new mysticism is emphasis on enlightenment… in this earthly life the mystics speak about a high and lofty wisdom— *sophia or sapentia*—which is the fruit of love and the gift of the Spirit. And within this wonderful wisdom are enlightenments, awakenings, gifts of a God who momentarily reveals His ineffable beauty and goodness and the secrets of His love.